Contents

LittleBrother
B O O K S

Published 2023.
Little Brother Books Ltd, Ground Floor, 23 Southernhay East, Exeter, Devon, EX1 1QL
Printed in the United Kingdom
books@littlebrotherbooks.co.uk | www.littlebrotherbooks.co.uk
The Little Brother Books trademarks, logos, email and website addresses and the Games Warrior logo and imprint are sole and exclusive properties of Little Brother Books Limited.

Welcome to Minecraft

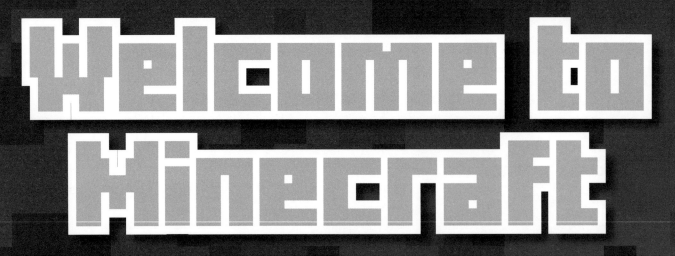

Whether you just want to build some really cool stuff, or embark on an epic adventure of survival and exploration, there's something for everyone in the wonderful world of Minecraft!

Since the very first block was mined way back in 2009, Minecraft has grown and evolved into one of the biggest games in the world – both in terms of its almost infinite worlds and also for the millions of people playing it around the planet. If you're reading this then you're most likely one of them, and whether you prefer the mining or the crafting side of the title, there's always something new to learn, and plenty more to come!

In the past couple of years we've seen the Caves & Cliffs two-part update expand the game world with even taller mountains and deeper mines, followed by the more recent Wild update that added new biomes, mobs and other fun items, including the ever-ominous Warden. The game's developer, Mojang, isn't showing any signs of taking a break, either, with the new 1.20 update bringing yet more features and gameplay opportunities for you to play with.

This year sees new default characters added to the game, giving Steve and Alex seven new friends that you can play as – and, of course, customise to make sure they look their very best! You'll also be able to find camels in the deserts, that can be tamed and ridden by two players at the same time.

Plus, you'll find fresh building blocks to give your next creation a different look with a new bamboo wood set. This includes a unique mosaic block and a cool new bamboo raft that works just like a boat. You'll also be able to place the new hanging signs around your base, while the chiselled bookshelves can be used to store your enchanted books and in-game journals. And it needn't end there, with Mojang sure to add even more content throughout 2023 and beyond!

MOB VOTE WINNER!

Also new for 2023 is the winner of the Minecraft LIVE event Mob Vote, which saw the seed-hunting sniffer edge out the tuff golem and rascal as the most popular choice and all set to find a new home in the game!

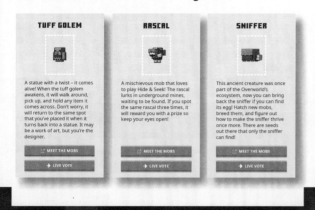

TUFF GOLEM

A statue with a twist – it comes alive! When the tuff golem awakens, it will walk around, pick up, and hold any item it comes across. Don't worry, it will return to the same spot that you've placed it when it turns back into a statue. It may be a work of art, but you're the designer.

⊡ MEET THE MOBS
→ LIVE VOTE

RASCAL

A mischievous mob that loves to play Hide & Seek! The rascal lurks in underground mines, waiting to be found. If you spot the same rascal three times, it will reward you with a prize so keep your eyes open!

⊡ MEET THE MOBS
→ LIVE VOTE

SNIFFER

This ancient creature was once part of the Overworld's ecosystem, now you can bring back the sniffer if you can find its egg! Hatch new mobs, breed them, and figure out how to make the sniffer thrive once more. There are seeds out there that only the sniffer can find!

⊡ MEET THE MOBS
→ LIVE VOTE

BAMBOO PAGODA

So, whether you're a newcomer to the limitless possibilities of Minecraft, or a seasoned veteran of the biggest builds and deepest mines, there's always something new to learn. Over the following pages, we'll guide new 'crafters through the essentials, round-up some of the newer content and key features to take your gaming to the next level, and offer up loads of useful tips and ideas for your next great adventure along the way!

CHISELLED BOOKSHELF

MORE WAYS TO PLAY

The original Minecraft is often referred to as the 'vanilla' game, as there have been several other Minecraft games released since – with 2023 seeing the launch of the Minecraft Legends.

Minecraft Legends (2023): Fun on your own but even better with friends, Legends is an action-based strategy game that lets you lead the fightback against an army of piglins threatening to destroy the Overworld.

Minecraft: Education Edition (2022): Although it's been in a Beta mode since 2016, this school-friendly version of the main game was formally launched last September. It contains loads of pre-planned lessons and exclusive resources (such as the Frozen Planet II tie-in) to help make learning a lot more fun by turning Minecraft into a classroom!

Minecraft Dungeons (2020): Turning the thrill of raiding an underground stronghold into a full-on game, Dungeons is still getting plenty of new updates, including a new multiplayer mode with online/couch co-op, new animals and extra missions to play.

Minecraft Earth (2019): This augmented reality (AR) spin-off game for mobile platforms quite literally dropped you into the game world, with the option to team up online for some huge builds - although support for the game officially ended in June 2021.

Minecraft: Story Mode (2015): The clue is in the name for this one, with an episodic action-adventure series developed by Telltale Games that lets you play as new character Jesse in a battle to save the Overworld. A second (and currently final) season was released in 2017 and it was even on Netflix until the end of 2022!

CREATIVE MODE

This mode opens up pretty much everything that Minecraft has to offer from the very beginning. Nearly all of the game's many items, tools and building blocks are unlocked and ready to use, so the only thing stopping you from building whatever you like is your imagination! You don't have to worry about enemies or health bars, and can even fly around the world for super-fast exploration (especially if you equip the elytra wings). If you just want to build cool stuff with minimal fuss, this is the place to start.

TIP!
You can't earn trophies or achievements in Creative Mode regardless, so there's no harm in toggling a few cheats to your advantage if you need them!

CHOOSE A MODE

There's more than one way to experience Minecraft, with several different options to get you started...

SURVIVAL MODE

If you prefer a real challenge, and more of a genuine 'gaming' experience, then Survival Mode is your go-to starting point. It's an epic adventure that demands plenty of mining and exploration, as you're dropped into a random world with a completely empty inventory, and face a very real threat from the many mobs that spawn in the shadows. You'll need to fight, heal, craft and upgrade – and that's just to get through the first few nights! As for beating the Wither and final Ender Dragon bosses, well that's going to take a LOT of time and effort...

HARDCORE MODE

This is only available for those playing the Java Edition (so not on consoles or handhelds), but it offers the ultimate challenge – Survival Mode with permadeath. In the normal game if you die you just risk losing your current inventory, in Hardcore Mode you lose all of your progress and have to start all over again. It's the ultimate Minecraft challenge, so good luck!

TIP! When setting up a new Survival game, toggle the switch for a bonus chest to spawn a few useful items to help get you through the first couple of nights.

MULTIPLAYER

Minecraft can be great fun on your own, but there are also many fun ways to hook up with friends. Not only can this make things more interesting, but having several people in the same game can make some of those bigger builds a whole lot easier. Although you can join any friend's adventure easily enough from the main game, there are also dedicated Realms servers which offer extra accessibility and features – but it does come with a monthly subscription, so it's only for the more dedicated community players.

MINECRAFT REALMS PLUS
Free 30-Day Trial, then £6.69/month

START FREE TRIAL

- Your Own Personal Realm Server– A Persistent World Always Online for You and Your Friends!
- Friends Play for Free in Your Realm
- Jump from Console to Mobile to PC – Any Device with Minecraft Marketplace
- Free Access to a Catalogue of 150+ Marketplace Packs
- Worlds on Your Realm Include Secure Backups
- Your First 30 Days Will be Free

UCKY BLOCK... clabs 490	Present Run By Blockception ★ 4.0 310	Winter Parkour By BBB Studios ★ 4.2 310	Desparia PVP/ By The Rage ★ 2.9
be magic... 660	Rising Lava Challenge By Dodo Studios ★ 4.2 830	Lucky Block Battle By Diveblocks ★ 4.5 830	Skyblock 100 By Team ★ 3.4

ADVENTURES AND MINI-GAMES

If you want a break from the main Minecraft experience, the Marketplace offers up a wealth of community-created experiences to try out. These provide a huge range of pre-built worlds and scenarios that can come with all sorts of restrictions or challenges in place to overcome – some might be tough, while others can be plain ridiculous! Most will come with a cost, though, so take care before you buy (and make sure you've got permission if someone else will be picking up the bill!).

SPECTATOR MODE

One of the newer features of Minecraft doesn't even require you to play the game. In Spectator Mode you can just fly around the map, not unlike in Creative Mode – only here you can't interact with the world, and instead 'ghost' through blocks if you try to land or fly into them. Similar to Hardcore Mode, it might also be unavailable in some Bedrock versions of the game.

JAVA VS BEDROCK: What's the Difference?

You might have heard of two different versions of the main Minecraft game and, while largely similar in terms of the core gameplay experience, there are some differences between them. The original PC version of the Minecraft game is now known as Minecraft: Java Edition, named after the computer code the game was built with. However, the latest gaming devices and consoles called for a new coding engine, and so the Bedrock Edition was created (built from the early Pocket Edition of the game).

The result is basically two versions of the same game, not unlike seeing a few differences between the PC and console versions of any other videogame. Java can be seen as the more detailed version, and may contain some elements that Bedrock doesn't have the tools for, such as some of the newer experimental content, more mods, and larger servers. However, if you're playing on a console, smartphone or tablet, then Bedrock will still have all of the core functionality you need to run super-smoothly, including the bonus of cross-platform play.

THE HEADS-UP

Everyone's got to start to somewhere, so here are some of the key features that newcomers will want to keep an eye on.

MASTER THE MOBS

The game's non-playable characters are known as mobs. Most of the animals will be passive unless you attack them, and the same applies to the villagers you'll find in the small hamlets scattered around the map. However, there are also many more aggressive mobs, especially those that spawn in the darker areas (at night or underground), along with the pillagers who are rather less-friendly locals – so you'll need to figure out the best way to deal with them.

WATCH YOUR HEALTH

In Survival Mode, if your health drops to zero, you'll die and have to respawn – either from the last bed you interacted with or your original starting point. Each of the 10 hearts can be halved, giving you 20 health points in total. Adding armour, which appears above your health bar, will reduce the amount of damage you take, while having a full hunger bar will cause any lost health to be replenished over time.

TIP!

Different foods provide varying nourishment rewards, while more complex recipes can even offer additional buffs – so give everything a taste!

EAT WELL

You won't need to eat a great deal to keep your hunger bar topped up (and you don't need to drink anything), but having a good food supply can be crucial to stay alive – as you'll need a full stomach to recover any lost health. Some simple food items include cooking dropped meat from dead animals, or finding apples and berries in the wild. Building a farm to grow a continuous crop of self-sustaining (and totally vegetarian) food is usually a smart move in Survival Mode.

QUICK CHANGE

You can equip up to nine items from your inventory into a hotbar that you can quickly access on the move. This means that you'll probably want to include the things you currently need, along with some key items you might need in a pinch – such as a sword to fend off a surprise attack, or some food for a quick health fix. You'll soon find your favourites, but it can help to have a system in place so you can get used to quickly jumping between common items without having to even look – such as a pickaxe and torches when mining.

Drop

GAIN EXPERIENCE

You can gain experience in the game by killing enemies and mining certain blocks, as well as crafting items and a few other in-game upgrades. Unlike many other games, you don't 'level up' your skills with XP; instead it's used as a currency which you can use to spend on repairs and enchantments. If you die you drop all of your XP and have to start over (unless you can return to the same spot and recover a small amount along with your lost loot), so spend it while you've got it!

TIP!

The axe is the second-best weapon after the sword, so having it next door can be a quick one-touch back-up if your sword breaks in a fight.

THE KEY FEATURES

A quick guide to some of the more common items and skills you'll need to become familiar with on your path to becoming a Minecraft master.

BUILDING BLOCKS

Everything in Minecraft is about blocks. Even things that don't look like the usual cubes, such as flowers or torches, count as a full-sized block, and there are a huge amount of differing types to play around with on your adventures.

One famous quirk of the game is that gravity doesn't always apply, which can look a bit weird, but you can also use this to your advantage and mine some blocks to leave others suspended in the air, and maybe even build a super base in the sky!

What blocks you choose to use may depend on what's nearby (which will typically mean lots of dirt and stone early on), or you might want your next build to have a certain look – perhaps using wood to build a cool log cabin, or trying out some really stylish designs in Creative Mode where everything is unlocked!

TIP!
Suspending jack o'lanterns a few blocks up in the air can be a great way to lead a clear and bright path back to your base.

ANTI-GRAVITY! NEED A LIFT?

CRAFTING

Outside of Creative Mode, in order to make and upgrade tools, you'll need to make a crafting table. They're easy to build (so don't be afraid to make lots of them!), and open up a wealth of new items depending on what you might have in your inventory. Of course, some of the best items require some very special, and often hard to find, ingredients to craft, but you'll have plenty of time to see what's on offer the more you play through the game – and it won't take long to get used to making those key tools and other day-to-day items.

TOOLS OF THE TRADE

There are a handful of key tools in Minecraft which you'll be using on a regular basis, and ideally looking to upgrade them using stronger materials. In Survival Mode they might start off quite simple, but over time you can make some super-powerful weapons and even add magical enchantments to make them even better!

The main tools are:

SWORD: Your main weapon in combat. Never leave home without one!

PICKAXE: Mines blocks and ore. The basic picks won't mine everything, though.

AXE: Use this for mining wood or quickly breaking down any wooden items.

SHOVEL: Like the pickaxe, but for digging dirt and other soft blocks like sand and gravel.

HOE: Farmers can use this to 'till', which is the technical term for preparing soil ready for planting crops.

The general upgrade path, with each new step adding more damage, power, or protection, is wood, stone, iron, diamond, and netherite. A stone pick is required to mine iron, an iron pick is needed to collect gold and redstone, and you'll have to upgrade to diamond to dig up obsidian. You can also make gold tools and armour but they tend to be weaker than their value might suggest, so you might want to save that gold for something else. Also some tools will have secondary uses, such as using the axe to peel bark from a tree, or making a path with the shovel, so keep an eye out for the on-screen prompts!

BASE BUILDING

Building a home can be great fun in Creative Mode, while a good base can be crucial to staying safe in Survival. This can be anything from making a simple hole in the ground or side of a mountain as a quick-fix hideout to get you through those first few dangerous nights, to building a huge castle or towering mansion to store all of your loot. If you're a keen explorer looking to travel all over your game world, you'll want to make a number of smaller bases at fairly regular intervals, to give you a place to quickly restock your tools and stay safe when the mobs come out at night. Besides adding some of the same key items (such as a crafting table), there's no right or wrong way to build a base, so feel free to play around with an underground stronghold, or maybe use a cave or some other natural in-game backdrops to save you half the building work!

ESSENTIAL ITEMS

Once you've mastered the basics of Minecraft, you'll soon
find some other key items that are worth keeping an eye on.
Here are just a few of them...

SEE THE LIGHT

Most of the more aggressive mobs in Minecraft spawn in low-light areas. This means they'll continuously spawn in caves and underground areas, and they'll also start appearing on the surface as soon as the sun begins to set – so it's a good idea to stay aware of your surroundings. If you're playing with the day-night cycle on, each day lasts for 20 minutes, of which only half is daylight. If you're above ground, tracking the movement of the sun can give you a decent idea of the time, and if it's dipping towards the horizon, it might be time to head for safety before the mobs come out to play!

You can stop mobs from spawning by placing torches and other light sources around, so keeping your home base well lit is always a good idea. Likewise, if you're mining underground, you'll want to scatter torches around as much as you can so you don't spend more time fighting than you do digging up the precious ore!

TIP: You can also use the sun as a compass. Just like the real world, it rises in the east and sets in the west, so by checking the direction it's moving in you'll know which way you're facing.

TIP: If you die, you get 5 minutes to return to the location and recover all of your dropped gear. Alternatively, you can toggle the settings when setting up the game to keep everything and save yourself the trouble.

SLEEP TIGHT

Not only are beds a handy tool for sleeping through the night and avoiding those pesky mobs, but they also double up as a respawn point. If you get killed in the game, you'll be resurrected back at the last bed you slept in (or just interacted with). If you don't have a bed, or it gets destroyed, you'll instead return to your original spawn point, which is why it's always a good idea to build a base near your starting location! If you're venturing out to explore or travelling around the game world, you'll want to have a good supply of beds in place, so if things do go wrong, you won't respawn too far away.

KNOW YOUR TABLES

We've already mentioned crafting and cover cartography tables below, but there are several similar items that you'll want to put to good use if you're looking to make the most from your Minecraft adventure. The furnace will be one of your more common tools, used to cook raw food ready for eating, and turn your metal ore into precious bars – as well as giving you the option to convert existing blocks into something new, such as cobblestone into a smoother stone finish, or turning sand into glass.

Another useful addition to your base would be an anvil. As with a grindstone, they can be used to repair your tools, but the anvil will also keep any enchantments in place (the enchanting table being something we'll come to later), and can even be used to combine two similar enchanted items into one even more potent new one! Later in the game (after you've spent at least a little time in the Nether) you can use a smithing table to upgrade diamond tools and armour to the toughest material in the game: netherite.

MAKE A MAP

Given that each created Minecraft world can be entirely new, not to mention huge, if you're planning on travelling around a bit, then having a good map or two can be a handy way to avoid getting lost. They're easily made using paper and with a cartography table you can expand them to cover an increasingly large area – with up to four size upgrades on offer. Your crafting location determines where the map begins, which does mean that the game world will continue beyond the edges of the map, so you can wander off it!

The maps will always be created with north at the top, while incorporating a compass to make a locator map will not only show your precise location, but also the direction you're facing at the time, which can be a great help in finding your way back home again.

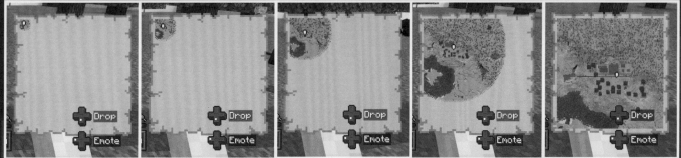

ESSENTIAL SKILLS

The clue might be in the name for some of the main gameplay features of Minecraft, but there are a few others you might want to focus on!

MINING

Unless you're playing in Creative Mode, you'll need to spend a lot of time mining in order to gather all of the resources you'll need to make progress. Plus, you'll want a steady supply of the likes of coal and iron in order to stay well-stocked with torches and the tools you'll need to mine some of the rarer blocks.

Every game world will have some natural paths into the deeper reaches of the map to get you started. A little trial and error exploring the various tunnels and caves in any area can be well worth the time and save you a lot of work. Alternatively, you might want to dig out your own path, typically from a main base to save too much travelling.

You can find your own favoured method, but the likes of a descending staircase with exploratory offshoots every 10 levels or so can be a good option, while keeping an eye out for natural tunnels and cave networks. Either way be prepared for a fight as any mobs you encounter are unlikely to be friendly!

TIP!
Take care not to get lost when mining. Using signs, differing torch layouts or just digging out a clean and tidy path can help you keep track of the route back to the surface.

ENCHANTING

To really take your inventory to the next level, the enchanting table can be used to add a variety of abilities to your tools and armour. You can upgrade the table by surrounding it with up to 15 bookcases, which need to be placed with a one-block gap but will give you access to increasingly more powerful enchantments. To use the table, you just need to place the item you want to enchant in the first slot and some of the blue lapis lazuli ore in the other. Your choice of enchantments will be limited, and dependent on how much XP you have, it might take a few tries to get the perfect combination for your needs – but the perks are nearly always worth it, so be sure to upgrade your gear whenever you can!

FARMING

To help ensure a good and sustainable, supply of food to keep you healthy, it can be useful to build a farm near any large home or base. You can plant seeds to grow wheat and craft it into bread, while other foods such as carrots, potatoes, melons and more can make for a tasty treat, or be combined into varying recipes. Farming typically works on expanding returns, so planting a single carrot will grow between two and four more – replant those and you'll have your very own supermarket in no time!

As well as food, you can also tame and keep animals to provide a good supply of meat, as well as the likes of milk, wool and eggs. You can breed more animals by feeding two of the same their favourite foods to put them into 'love mode' and they'll spawn a new infant. You don't need to worry about keeping your furry friends fed, though you might want to build some fences to stop them from wandering off!

WHAT'S THEIR FAVOURITE FOOD?

CHICKENS	Seeds
COWS	Wheat
FOXES	Sweet berries
HORSES	Golden apples
OCELOTS	Raw cod or raw salmon
PANDAS	Bamboo
PARROTS	Seeds
PIGS	Carrots, potatoes or beetroot
RABBITS	Carrots or dandelions
SHEEP	Wheat
WOLVES	Bones (to tame) and any raw meat

TIP!
Crops need water to grow, which can filter through up to four blocks in any direction – which means a single block of water in the middle can sustain a 9x9 grid.

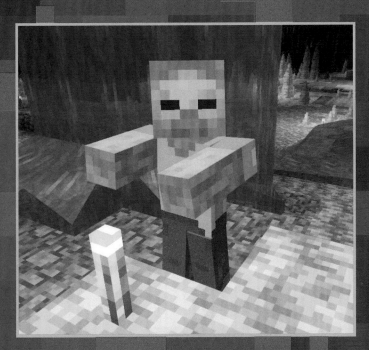

COMBAT

Unless you're playing in Creative Mode or on Peaceful difficulty, combat can be more of an enforced skill that you'll need to get to grips with. Except for some boss battles, it's not overly complicated or difficult, but you'll need to take care you don't get ambushed by the explosive creepers or find yourself outnumbered. Look to use the environment to your advantage, such as using blocks or water streams to keep enemies at a safe distance, while a shield can be used to block a skeleton's arrows, and even deflect them back. Most importantly, don't be afraid to run away and find a safe place to heal up if your health bar is running low!

TIP!
Frogs can jump up to 8 blocks high, so if you want to keep a few close by a small fence might not be enough to stop them!

FROG CHORUS

Meet some of the game's newest mobs introduced in the recent Wild update, with frogs offering some unique features...

THE HIP HOPPER

You'll find frogs in swamp areas, including the new mangrove swamps that were added to the game in the Wild update. They're mostly passive (as long as you leave them alone) and will happily jump around on land or across lily pads, as well as being fast movers in the water. They come in three different colours, which changes based on the biome they grow up in – with green frogs appearing in colder climates, white frogs in warmer regions, and an orange version in more temperate landscapes.

If they do come under attack, they'll use their long tongues to pull enemies close in (which can make mobs instantly disappear), but there's no real benefit in killing them yourself, except for the small XP boost. Plus, they have a taste for slimes, so if you happen to be in an area where those green blobs are spawning, having a few frogs around can be a big help!

FEEDING AND BREEDING

As mentioned, frogs enjoy snacking on a slime or two, which you can exploit with the slimeballs harvested from dead slimes. You can use them to get frogs to follow you around, while feeding them to frogs will put them into love mode. One fun fact for this new arrival, is that frogs are the first mob not to simply spawn a smaller version of themselves. Instead, they'll head to a nearby water source and lay some frogspawn, which will eventually hatch into tadpoles and swim around for a while before turning into frogs.

This does give you a small window of opportunity to rehouse (and recolour) some frogs. Using a bucket, you can scoop up tadpoles and carry them around in your inventory – so you can head off to a different biome and set them free, where the frogs will grow up in whatever colour suits their new surroundings.

FROGLIGHTS

These are a great new addition to your lighting options, but they're not easy to get hold of outside of Creative Mode. They're made when frogs eat a magma cube – but as these are only found in the Nether, you'll need to find a way to take some frogs through a portal and into the underworld (perhaps using a lead or luring them with slimeballs).

Like slimes, magma cubes get smaller with each few hits, and frogs will only eat the smallest form, so you might need some careful sword work to trim them down to size. When a frog does eat a magma cube, a froglight will drop in its place, with the colour of the light reflecting the colour of the frog. As well as looking cool, froglights also boast the maximum light rating of 15, so they should help to brighten up any location!

ALLAY

Joining the similarly passive frogs as part of the Wild update you'll find some other cute new companions who can lend a helping hand...

The trick with the allay is that any item you give them they'll then seek out and collect for you – but they can't mine and will only pick up things already lying around, which does limit their use a little. However, if you're mining for ore or harvesting crops and only want certain things picked up, they can happily help out.

On freeing them, don't worry too much about what you give them to hunt for – but if you don't give them something they won't follow you around and will eventually fly away. In the same way, if you get bored of having them around, just take their equipped item away from them and they'll stop following you.

Winner of the 2021 Mob Vote, the allay is an adorable flying addition to Minecraft's friendlier natives, and is happy to follow you on your travels and help to gather up some dropped items. However, the angrier mobs don't seem to like them too much, as you'll find them caged up in pillager outposts or trapped in a cell in a woodland mansion – so you'll have to break them free first! You only need to smash up enough of their cage or cell for them to fly out, and if you want to keep them as a companion you'll need to give them something from your inventory.

Typically, the allay will drop any found items within a block or two of your feet. However, one fun feature is that they love music, so if you build a note block and activate it to play a note, they'll head towards it and drop off any items there. Also, if you play a music disc on a nearby jukebox it can break into a cute little dance!

WARDEN

Unlike the other new arrivals, this is one big bad mob that you'll be better off avoiding completely!

The Warden isn't so much a boss, more of a super-strong deterrent that is best avoided at almost all costs. The reason is that it can inflict massive damage in a single hit – enough to kill anyone without the strongest armour – so you don't really want to get into a fight with one, as it's designed to be more like a movie monster you'd want to run away from. The good news is that they only appear in the sculk-filled Deep Dark biomes, and are also almost totally blind.

TIP!
The Warden will investigate where projectiles land, so you can fire arrows or throw snowballs to lure it away from you.

You'll trigger a Warden if you alert a few sculk shrieker blocks, which will cause the Warden to burrow up from its underground lair. Because it relies on its sense of sound and vibrations, the more you can limit your own movement by sneaking or simply staying still, the better, and it will eventually dig back underground after a minute of silence – although it will also target other mobs if anything else is unlucky enough to catch its attention.

It can inflict the new Darkness effect, which risks making it even harder to see where it is. If you are hiding away, you can listen out for its chest pulsing to get a sense of its location and how close it is (the pulse gets quicker the more suspicious it gets), while flickering lights are also a hint that it's close. It has 500 health points if you do fancy a fight, but the chances are that if you go toe-to-toe with a Warden it's not going to end well for you...

17

MONSTER HUNT

Do you know your enemy? Figure out the hostile mobs from the clues to complete the line-up, with the coloured squares providing the letters to unravel an anagram for a bonus baddie!

TEST YOUR MINECRAFT KNOWLEDGE ON FACTS YOU'VE LEARNT IN THIS ULTIMATE GUIDE!

Across

2. A spell-binding enemy who can be a wizard with potions.

3. This eight-legged mob spends its spare time on the web.

7. The walking undead?

9. A flying foe who could also be a 'menace' in Star Wars...

10. You'll find this spooky, er, man in the End.

12. Flying around the Nether, it sounds a bit like a ghost...

13. A lot like a villager, but not quite so friendly.

15. Lives in the End, and makes for very handy boxes.

16. Fires arrow from afar when they have a bone to pick with you.

Down

1. A gooey cube that's maybe more 'lime' than green.

4. This Nether-dweller prefers gold to oinking.

5. Because zombies can't breathe underwater...

6. More of a boar than a piglin, but it 'hogs' the spotlight!

8. Found floating in the Nether, it sounds fire-y!

11. A favourite food for frogs to make froglights.

14. This special zombie type can be found in sunny desert regions.

Bonus Baddie

Answers on page 48.

THE DEEP DIVE

Can you find these recent additions to the game hidden in the grid?
As in the new Deep Dark biome, they might be hard to spot as they can be
found in any direction, including backwards and diagonally!

```
Y T I C T N E I C N A P M T E
D A R K N E S S R R C W S N C
D N R O H T A O G X C Y T P H
Y E A T S C V S U M L Q S M O
K A E A H Y R V C A B D E A S
S A L P F E Q W T U F C H W H
E N E L S X W A L R L K C S A
L I I N A L C A O I C K H E R
O X F Y S W A G R I H R T V D
P Y T N I T S T R D I M I O S
D Z E B K P F B E E E N W R E
A C D Z A S D I K L A N T G N
T T D W F U N E W L Q S A N S
H B N M M A R N J S R J O A O
P A C K E D M U D J Q L B M R
```

ALLAY	ECHO SHARD	SCULK
ANCIENT CITY	FROGSPAWN	SENSOR
BOAT WITH CHEST	GOAT HORN	SHRIEKER
CATALYST	MANGROVE SWAMP	SWIFT SNEAK
DARKNESS	MUD BRICK	TADPOLES
DEEPSLATE	PACKED MUD	

There's also a hidden word buried away
that we haven't listed, but we're not
sure if you'll want to find it anyway...

Answers on page 48.

GETTING CREATIVE

Creative Mode gives you all the freedom you need, both to build big and also to master some of the trickier skills...

ANYTHING GOES

The big question with Creative Mode is probably: 'What should I build?'. Given that your options are limited only by your imagination, along with all of the fun tools at your disposal, there's no simple answer. Creative Mode is often a place for larger and often more complicated builds, and a quick look online will throw up hundreds of great ideas, from cool automated mechanisms, to recreations of famous locations, or even entire cities.

If you're new to the game, then you might want to start small. Perhaps try to recreate your own home or look to build everyday items on a larger scale, such as a giant car, a towering lighthouse or some fun animal shapes. You can take advantage of your invincibility to freely explore underwater locations and perhaps build an undersea base, or fly up to the skies to create a huge airship from which you can look out across your game world.

ACCESS ALL AREAS

Playing in Creative Mode comes with two very notable advantages. Firstly, pretty much every item in the game is unlocked from the very beginning and with an infinite supply – so there's no messing around having to gather resources. Secondly, you're invincible, so you don't have to worry about mobs (who'll leave you alone anyway), or falling into lava or even drowning, which leaves you free to focus purely on having fun. As an added bonus, you can double-tap the jump button to fly, which gives you super-fast navigation around the map!

TRY NEW THINGS!

FROG HOUSE

INTERIOR DESIGN

EARLY FOUNDATIONS

SECRET ROOF DEN...

FEELS LIKE HOME!

NEW AND IMPROVED

With the fully unlocked and endless inventory, Creative Mode can also be a great place to try new things or brush up on your skills. You can destroy all blocks as quickly as you can build them, so feel free to mix and match all manner of different items to see what you can combine for a cool new look, or experiment with items that you might not have used before.

It also gives you the freedom to try new things to make your creations look more realistic, such as adding curves. You can also use slabs, steps and other tricks to make your build look less 'blocky', and trying different lighting combinations can lead to some dazzling visuals. Creative Mode is a playground, so have fun with it!

SURVIVAL TRAINING

Even if Survival Mode is your go-to gameplay choice, there's plenty of merit in having a creative world to dip into. It can be a place to try out different things or to see what you can do with any newly-found blocks or unlocked items, without draining those valuable resources – such as using the new mangrove logs to see how a huge wooden cabin with a treehouse might look (perhaps one complete with a secret den hidden in the attic that can only be accessed through a trapdoor in the roof, with a nearby target block for some crossbow practice!).

Creative Mode is also a great way to play around with the varying effects of redstone with easy access to the likes of pistons and observers, or to see for yourself how to mix up the many potions or enchantments on offer. Then, when you head back to Survival Mode you should have a better idea of what you might want to be building next, but without that element of trial-and-error that can drain your inventory.

HELPING HANDS

Minecraft can be easy to learn but tricky to master. Fortunately, there's no shortage of resources around where you can find help and inspiration.

MINECRAFT

MINECRAFT.NET

It might not have the kind of content you'll find on YouTube, and certainly not the same kind of quantity, but the Minecraft website is a great place to stay up-to-date with all of the latest developments. With the game continuing to drip-feed new content (with many small updates alongside the bigger ones), you'll find the key headlines joined by some nice blog-style content to help explain the basics of what's new and how it works.

You can also use the site as your out-of-game Marketplace, with easy access to the latest downloadable content (DLC) as well as a Community page covering some of the fan events and other fun activities you might want to join in with. And, of course, it caters for the full Minecraft portfolio, so if you're also interested in Dungeons or Legends, then the site has you covered!

MINECRAFT: EDUCATION EDITION

With its own homepage (education.minecraft.net), the growing Education Edition set-up has a number of great ways to broaden your horizons within a Minecraft world. It looks to combine the fun of gaming and the literal building blocks put in place by Minecraft to make education projects even more interesting – for both students and teachers alike!

This includes more than 600 pre-designed lessons, and the chance to make up your own projects with the tools provided. You'll also find crossovers into the main game, such as the Frozen Planet II DLC that launched in 2022, letting you navigate the icy wilderness both as an explorer and as some of the local wildlife – so you could play as a polar bear or killer whale, while also learning about their lives and natural habitats!

PLAY THE WAY YOU WANT
Playing Minecraft on your favorite devices is so easy! And so fun!

YOUTUBE & TWITCH

If you're reading this then the chances are you'll already have seen a fair number of video clips, tutorials and gameplay compilations, and YouTube remains the largest library of Minecraft support you'll find. There aren't too many questions you won't find answered in a video, along with a near-endless supply of great ideas to try...

whether that takes a few minutes to learn or a two-hour walkthrough to replicate!

Of course, some outlets may be more useful than others depending on what you're after. Some YouTube channels, and the growing number of Twitch streamers, may focus more on the personality of the person behind the controller;

while others may prefer to take a more slow-paced and detailed approach to any given situation, or may target younger or older gamers. All of which means that there's no clear-cut 'best' online resource, but with plenty to choose from you should be able to find at least a few that suit your style!

TOP TUBERS

The official channel may not be the most popular, and not all of these will be posting as regularly as they have done, with a few targeting other games as well – but here are some of the biggest Minecraft YouTubers of recent years...

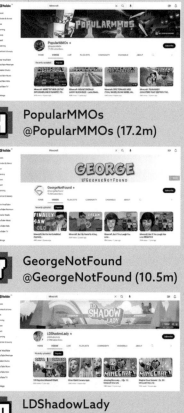

1 Official YouTube @Minecraft (10.6m subscribers)

2 Dream @dream (31.2m)

3 DanTDM @DanTDM (21.4m)

4 PopularMMOs @PopularMMOs (17.2m)

5 TommyInnit @TommyInnit (11.8m)

6 Stampylonghead @stampycat (10.6m)

7 GeorgeNotFound @GeorgeNotFound (10.5m)

8 Mumbo Jumbo @ThatMumboJumbo (8.5m)

9 Grian @grian (7.9m)

10 LDShadowLady @ldshadowlady (6.9m)

NEW ITEMS

As well as adding some new biomes, the recent Wild update also dropped several other fresh options for your inventory.

NEW LOCATIONS

We'll cover some of the specifics a bit later, but the Wild update added three new locations ready for you to explore. The mangrove swamp is a rather more claustrophobic twist on the standard swamp, with the mangrove trees hiding their trunks within a sprawling system of leaves, vines and roots. This can make them tricky to navigate, but they can also be sculpted to your advantage to help keep enemies at bay.

The Deep Dark is a new underground biome, which is coated in a green substance known as sculk, which can also form the rare but very impressive-looking ancient cities that are best found under large mountain ranges. The good news is that your usual mobs don't spawn in these areas and there can be some epic loot chests to find. However, the bad news is they're usually poorly lit and if you make too much noise then you might just spawn one of most dangerous mobs of all: the Warden.

DARKNESS EFFECT

24

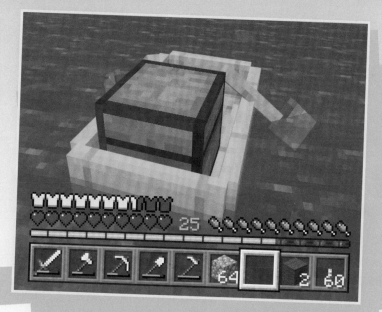

make a clearly recognisable sound from quite a distance – and with eight variants to collect you can either use them to attract the attention of others, or maybe even to team up and play a tune!

One of the new features of the ancient cities are the echo shards that can be crafted to make a recovery compass. This can be used after you die to help guide you towards where any dropped loot will have fallen and maybe save some of your best gear, but you will still need to move fast before it's gone for good.

NEW ITEMS

Among the other new additions are some that might prove more useful than others, depending on how you play the game. Explorers may appreciate the boat with a chest, which pretty much lives up to its name – but being able to load up a boat with many more items beyond your personal inventory can make for a great way to move quickly around the map or head out to distant islands, and with a good supply of materials at hand ready for when you head ashore.

The goat horn is more of a fun addition, especially for those playing with friends. It's dropped when a goat runs into a hard surface and can be used to

NEW TRICKS

One very handy addition for your deep dark travels is the Swift Sneak enhancement, which speeds up your movement when crouched – something you'll likely need to be doing a lot of to keep the Warden at bay. Applied to leggings it can boost your sneaking speed by up to 75%, but the downside is that you can't create it yourself, and so you'll need to find it in an enchanted book in an ancient city.

Not quite so helpful is the new temporary negative effect called Darkness. This can be triggered by sculk shriekers or when you're close to the Warden and clouds the screen in a creepy fog that only the brightest light sources can cut through. Having this reduced visibility in an already dark location can make plotting a path to safety that much trickier, so it can pay to simply hide up and wait it out.

WHAT'S IN STORE?

With a wealth of new looks, challenges and entire game worlds on offer, there's loads of fresh content on the Minecraft Marketplace!

The Marketplace may come with a slightly different look and content based on the version of the game you're playing, but you'll find it split into several handy sections. You should also be able to use a side bar or pop-up selection offering quick access to new arrivals, popular content, Realms multiplayer templates and more, as well as your existing library of downloads.

A PRICE TO PAY?

Of course, not everything is going to be free, and the Marketplace uses its own unique 'Minecoin' currency which you can buy in various quantities starting from a few hundred for a little under £2 (with the game highlighting the closest option required for your next purchase in cash if you click straight through to what you want to buy). While it might not seem like a lot at first, some content will cost a lot more and by the time you've bought a few new skins, a couple of mini-games and the latest superhero DLC, it can quickly add-up. So always make sure that if you're not picking up the tab yourself, you've got clear permission to make each and every purchase.

If you're new to the game and not really sure where to look among the hundreds of options, you might want to focus on some of the free content to get a feel for what's on offer without losing out. Minecraft (courtesy of its developer, Mojang) has been adding its own steady supply of ready-made downloads over the years, while you'll also find lots of community creations for free.
It's a good way to find out what kind of things you might like, or what could improve your personal Minecraft experiences, so when you do splash the cash you'll know it's something that you'll really benefit from and not regret half an hour later.

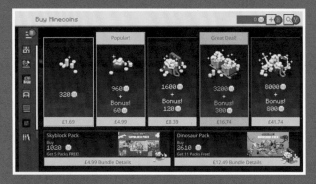

TIP!

To help find the free content, use the search filter option and scroll down to sort the listings by price from low to high – so all the free content will appear at the top!

SKIN & TEXTURE PACKS

These can be great ways to change how your world looks, by transforming the appearance of the characters, mobs, and even the blocks themselves. There are almost no limits on what you can dress mobs up as, and you'll find skin packs for all occasions, from Christmas outfits to your favourite football team or popular film and TV characters.

Similarly, texture packs can offer an entirely new look for the game. By changing the visual style of blocks and creating entire locations with them, you can set your next adventure in a whole new world – and the possibilities are almost endless. From ancient civilisations to futuristic sci-fi landscapes and just about everything in-between, including plenty of mash-ups with iconic pop culture franchises (and, of course, some great videogame crossovers), Minecraft may never look the same again!

TIP!

If you're into rather more homely builds, you'll also find furniture packs which can be used to give your interiors a stylish new appearance.

Shadow Mobs
By Mob Pie
★ 4.7   160

ADVENTURES & MINI-GAMES

These come under the 'Worlds' banner, and offer up a rich variety of pre-built Minecraft adventure maps and survival spawns that you either have fun with or perhaps test yourself to overcome their unique challenges.

As for the mini-games, pretty much anything goes. If you can imagine it, there's a fair chance someone has had a crack at making it happen! And, again, you can expect plenty of well-known films, cartoons and other famous characters to make an appearance...

Of course, Minecraft does have its limitations which means that a lot of what's on the Marketplace can be a little hit-and-miss in terms of gameplay, but there's certainly no shortage of creative content to explore. So, again, if you're new to it maybe play around with the free stuff to see what you might like and perhaps find some trusted creators, and always do a little research before splashing out on anything a little more expensive!

TIP!
Leather shoes will stop you sinking into soft snow, while equipping any piece of leather armour will also prevent Freeze Damage.

TOUGH TERRAIN

Not all of Minecraft's many biomes come with easy access to food, wood and other resources, but they can hold some great rewards if you're ready to brave the elements.

UNDERWATER

Due to the obvious breathing difficulties with exploring the oceans, this is probably something to consider a little later in the game. The main way to extend your oxygen levels long enough to be able to do anything of note is with a potion for Water Breathing – which gives you three minutes as standard or up to eight minutes if you mix in some redstone. However, unless you find some on your travels, you'll need to gather the required blaze powder and Nether wart ingredients from a trip to the Nether.

Other shorter solutions include a Respiration enchantment, or perhaps some turtle shell headgear. One useful feature is a conduit, which enables players to keep breathing for as long as you stay within in its range

SNOW

There are many varying types of snowy biome, and while some will have trees, many will not. Others might be packed with ice blocks and little else, so you won't find much in terms of handy food sources, besides a few rabbits. The polar bears are largely passive and cute to look at, but they can be easily provoked and cause a lot of damage, so approach with care! Hostile mobs may be more scattered but are still a threat, with the stray variant of the skeleton wrapped up in torn clothes.

The cold isn't a big issue, although if you fall down into powdered snow sections you can take Freeze Damage. You will find that water can freeze in these biomes, which does make it easy to cross a large river, and you can even farm ice blocks using the Silk Touch enchantment to build 'roads' you can sail boats on. However, it's not great for farming, and so to keep any crops watered, you'll need to place torches or other light/heat sources nearby, and maybe add a roof covering to help keep the cold at bay.

If you're just starting out, you might want to head towards a greener neighbouring biome to find a place you can return to for some essentials, such as wood and good food supplies. When you do get to explore, look out for igloos which can hide an underground stash, while snow-topped mountains can hold lots of great resources, including emeralds.

(as well as buffing your mining speed and damaging nearby mobs) – but the required crafting ingredients can be hard to find.

Until you're able to get your hands on some nautilus shells and the rare 'heart of the sea' needed to build a conduit, placing items such as doors or signs can sometimes create a small air pocket you can use to catch your breath again (though it might not work as well on all versions of the game) – with doors also stopping water from flowing into a room or other space.

It's a trick you can use to get started on an underwater build, or maybe you can drop gravity-affected blocks down from above the surface. Simply digging a few blocks into a cliff and dropping a door behind you can also work for a quick starting point. If water does flow in, you can use sponges to soak it up, but if you don't have any just be sure you've plugged any holes, then fill the 'wet' space with soft blocks (such as sand) and remove them again to get rid of any unwanted water.

TIP!
Working underwater can slow things down, but equipping the Aqua Affinity enchantment can speed up your mining and save valuable time.

29

DESERT

Similarly to snowy regions, desert biomes will be short on wood and you won't find too many animals around should you need to top up your health or hunger bars – although the dead bushes scattered around will give you a good supply of sticks to make tools with. The upside is that these areas will often have a good number of buildings which are good for looting, and villages to help pick up some of those essential supplies. Enemies will still appear, with the husk featuring as a zombie variant that can survive in daylight, but with the largely open landscape you should be able to see them coming from some way off. Plus, the often flat areas that make up a desert biome can provide a great foundation for building on.

When it comes to mining, you might find lush caves under the more mountainous deserts areas. You may also want to look out for the badlands biome, which is easily identifiable with its red sand and multi-coloured terracotta blocks. As well as letting you make for some great-looking builds, these colourful regions can also house a lot of pre-built mines, complete with rails, loot chests and a good supply of wooden planks, offering up a perfect place for a base. As with the snowy biomes, if you're starting out you might want to look for nearby plains or savannah biomes that can be a good place to build a farm or two to keep you restocked ahead of your next sandy expedition.

LETTER BOXES

Think you know your 9x tables... but with words?
Each grid hides a nine-letter word or two-word phrase
that starts with the circled letter and moves one letter
at a time in any direction (but not diagonally).

You'll also discover the first letter of each answer
provides an anagram to reveal another bonus 9-letter
word that unites them all!

TEST YOUR
MINECRAFT KNOWLEDGE
ON FACTS YOU'VE
LEARNT IN THIS
ULTIMATE GUIDE!

1

A	H	S
R	H	O
D	C	Ⓔ

2

L	G	Ⓕ
I	O	R
G	H	T

3

Ⓘ	R	M
N	O	E
G	O	L

4

Ⓜ	I	N
F	A	E
T	H	S

5

I	W	E
T	Ⓣ	H
H	E	R

6

M	P	A
O	S	S
Ⓒ	E	S

7

T	O	R
Ⓐ	A	C
V	I	T

8

I	R	E
T	E	H
Ⓝ	E	T

9

M	L	Ⓡ
O	A	A
N	S	W

Bonus word _____

MINEDLE

It's like Wordle but for all things Minecraft! Can you find the friendly
mobs, based on these words? A black box is the wrong letter, a green one
is correct, and yellow shows a required letter that's in the wrong place!
We've done the first one to get you started.

1 G H O S T → G O A T S

2 S M A L L

3 S T O R E

4 C A P E D

THE NETHER

Often thought of an as underground realm of the main 'Overworld', the Nether is actually an entirely separate dimension.

HOW TO GET THERE

You can build a portal anywhere within the Overworld using obsidian – which is found where lava and water meet, and can be mined with a diamond pickaxe. It can be as simple as a door frame-like shape that has a 2x3 gap in the middle, which can then be lit with fire or a flint & steel.

WHAT TO BE WARY OF

Pretty much everything, with a large amount of lava and little in the way of friendly mobs. The flying ghasts can cause a lot of damage with their fireballs, while Nether fortresses will have some tough blaze and wither skeleton enemies.

Your portal can be destroyed, so it can pay to make good use of any fireproof cobblestone you have to build a base around it. You can also use it to make indestructible paths to help you navigate, as maps and compasses don't work as normal in the Nether (or the End). Also note that beds will explode if you try to sleep in one, so be prepared to dip back to the Overworld often or look to build a respawn anchor.

WHAT TO LOOK FOR

The main goal may be to find those fortresses, along with bastion remnants, as they'll hold some of the best rewards which you might need for those boss fights. Plus, the warped forest biome will have a lot of Endermen if you need to farm Ender pearls for the End, with the likes of glowstone blocks, quartz and crying obsidian also proving very useful.

HOW TO SURVIVE

There's no water here, but you can get food from hoglins or just bring a good stash with you. There's no day/night cycle and unless you're mining you shouldn't need too many torches – but be wary of hidden lava blocks that might need to be quickly plugged with more cobblestone.

You can keep the otherwise aggressive piglins from bothering you by wearing a single piece of gold armour, and even trade with them by throwing a gold ingot in their direction. The striders you'll find wading through lava can also be used as mounts using a saddle and a warped fungus on a stick to control them, letting you safely cross the many large lava lakes.

One useful feature is that travelling one block in the Nether is the same as eight blocks in the Overworld, so you can set up a network of portals to help fast-travel around your game world!

TIP!
To farm more obsidian be sure to keep the water flowing towards the lava, rather than the other way around, as that only generates stone.

THE END

A surreal floating void in the stars, the End can live up to its name in Survival Mode...

HOW TO GET THERE

You'll need to find a portal in an underground stronghold and place an eye of Ender into each of the 12 blocks to fire it up. Just be aware, that you'll arrive in the presence of the Ender Dragon, and the only way out is to defeat the boss or die and respawn back in the Overworld – so make sure you're ready!

WHAT TO BE WARY OF

As the name suggests, you'll find a good number of Endermen scattered around. The only other enemy is a shulker, which disguises itself as a purple block in buildings and will fire projectiles that can track you (unless you hit, block, or dodge it). If you gather up their shulker shells, you can make a shulker box which works like a chest but remains as a single item when mined – so you can carry a full chest's worth of gear in a single inventory slot!

WHAT TO LOOK FOR

After defeating the Ender Dragon (more on her later!), a smaller gateway portal will appear to transport you to the distant biomes. On these outer islands you should search for the End cities, which are tower-like structures that may require a little platforming to reach the loot at the top.

As well as some good weapons and armour, you'll also find Ender chests (best mined with a Silk Touch-enchanted pickaxe) which acts like a cloud storage inventory unique to each player. If you can find a city with an End ship in tow, you can also bag yourself the elytra, which you can equip like a wingsuit to help you glide around the skies.

HOW TO SURVIVE

It's a dark place, but the sand-like End stone makes for a bright backdrop so you'll rarely need light sources of your own. Again, there's no water and food is in short supply, with your snacks mostly limited to the chorus fruit which teleports you up to eight blocks when you eat it, so make sure you're a safe distance from the void first!

Respawn anchors, as well as beds, will explode here, so if you die it's back to the Overworld. Unfortunately, Nether portals won't work in the End either, which means you can't build your own shortcuts – so be prepared for some long trips with high-risk, but potentially great, rewards!

TIP!
To access the gateway portals, you might need to throw an Ender pearl into one to teleport yourself inside, but they can be farmed by killing a few nearby Endermen.

MINECRAFT MECHANICS

With the help of some redstone and a little bit of planning, you can turn an ordinary build into an extraordinary one...

CLICK AND COLLECT

It doesn't take long to get used to building with blocks in Minecraft, but one of the game's best features is the almost endless possibilities that its more complicated mechanics can offer.

It needn't be hugely complex, with simple solutions using levers, buttons and pressure plates that can be directly linked to certain items. So you can start small and learn new tricks every day!

However, once you really get to grips with redstone dust, you can aspire to huge multi-layered and fully-automated contraptions that can revolutionise your world.

DIRECT CURRENCY

Redstone works like electricity, with triggers that spark a current that can be conducted by redstone dust (and powered by redstone torches). So, while a lever next to a door will open it without redstone, you can place them several blocks apart and link the two with a redstone dust trail to activate it.

By expanding on this simple premise, and adding in the likes of some clever gadgets such as redstone repeaters and comparators, along with useful blocks such as pistons, observers, and dispensers, things can certainly get a lot more creative with some amazing results.

THE BASICS

As an example, you can come up with a variety of ways to open a door. As mentioned, a lever next to it will work on its own, as will a pressure plate on the floor in front to save you any kind of interaction as you just walk up to the door and it will pop open for you... and also close itself!

TIP: Don't place pressure plates outside your doors unless you're sure that wandering mobs won't be able to get in!

A SIMPLE SOLUTION

You can expand upon the simple pressure plate idea, by adding sticky pistons to create a 'sliding door' effect. You'll need some redstone torches to act as a power source, but a simple redstone dust circuit underneath the build will trigger the pistons and pull the doors open (and then close them behind you). Keeping the workings hidden from view is a whole new trick to master!

TIP: Redstone dust still takes up a full block's worth of space, so you can't place a slab or other half-block to fill in the gap – so you might need to get creative to cover up your workings!

THE SMART DESIGN

This rather more complicated alternative (based on an old creation by @jankesaurous) adds redstone repeaters to help link the two doors on a loop, so that they both open at the same time. It also includes a 'lock' for the doors by adding in two secondary sticky pistons connected to a lever. Once activated they move a block on either side that will either complete or break the circuit – once broken the doors won't open, which means you can add pressure plates outside and still keep any mobs safely locked out!

TIP: The doors don't need to be glass blocks. You can use the same blocks as your wall, or even bookcases or stairs, to create hidden doorways and secret rooms!

THE RAIL WAY

One of the more fun, and not overly-complicated, ways to use redstone is to build your own minecart rail network. It's a great way to simply travel between locations, as well as for hauling goods from your mines.

Basic rails can be used on their own, as you can 'lean' into a minecart to give you some forward momentum, but adding in powered rails will have you speeding around your world and let you soak up the view!

The easiest way is to add two or three powered rails every 20 blocks or so. You can space them out by more than 30 blocks, but a shorter gap will help to keep your speed up as you slow down when travelling across unpowered tracks.

You'll need to place a redstone torch next to them as your power source, and will need to add more powered rails to help boost you up any slopes or hills, as you don't want to lose speed and roll back down!

You can also add 'T'-shaped junctions and place a lever nearby to flip the tracks to turn left or right, or build a 'Z'-shaped zig-zag to create a diagonal line. One neat trick is to add a small incline at the start/end of each line, with a powered rail linked to a button – so you can place your minecart on the slope, jump in, and then press the button to fire up the rail and get you off to a flying start! Or you can build a giant rollercoaster and ride it on a never-ending loop...

MANGROVE SWAMPS

With a new wood set and some interesting mud variations, this new biome offers up some cool new building options.

TIP!
One unique feature of mangrove trees is that the saplings, or 'propagules', are the first in the game that can be planted in blocks underwater.

MANGROVE TREES
You'll find the new mangrove swamps in high temperature and high humidity regions, so look out for dense tree-covered areas close to the likes of a desert or savannah biome. The towering mangrove trees can stand out from afar, as they can also be tightly packed together, causing the mangrove swamps to become cluttered with a network of roots and vines, as the mangrove trees aren't like your normal wood sources.

The unusual thing about them is that their trunks don't reach down to the ground, with the roots instead supporting it and the wooden blocks hidden away inside their leaves. This means that mining it for wood (to create mangrove planks and so on) can require some careful platforming but it does provide a cool coloured twist, with a distinctive crimson finish looking not unlike the older acacia trees.

Like a few similar blocks, mangrove can offer some contrasting looks depending on which way each block is facing when you place it, so you might want to pay careful attention if you want a clean-looking build. You can also use the wood to craft a rather more stylish mangrove boat. While you can harvest the leaves and roots to be used as building blocks, they're probably not something you'll have a lot of day-to-day use for, but they could still be included in some weird and wonderful designs!

MUD AND MORE!

We've seen mud in Minecraft before, but originally it was more of a liquid than a solid block, but now you can mine it like dirt in and around any mangrove swamp – or you can create your own by pouring water from a bottle onto a dirt block. Mud can be a little soft to walk on, so you may sink into it a little but it shouldn't slow you down.

There are several variations you can make using mud to give it a slightly more attractive look from its standard grey blocks. You can combine it with wheat to create packed mud blocks as a nice alternative building tool, while you can combine four of those packed mud blocks into a mud brick, which could make for an even better-looking build!

One additional trick is to place mud on top of pointed dripstone, which will drain the moisture from it and turn the block into clay (which can then be turned in terracotta or clay bricks) – so while mud might not be one of the more attractive blocks in the game, it certainly adds a good number of building options!

TIP!
Much like sand, mud can also be used as an alternative to dirt for planting sugar cane and bamboo.

THE DEEP DARK

In the deeper, darker corners of Minecraft's lowest levels a strange green substance can be found in an all-new biome...

THE INCREDIBLE SCULK

The Deep Dark biome is rare, but if you wanted to search it out, you've a better chance looking underground near mountainous areas. You won't find much water or lava around, but you will find the toughened reinforced deepslate. As for the strangely sparkly green stuff that makes the Deep Dark quickly recognisable, that's known as sculk.

It's looks like more of a coating than a block in itself, but that's not to say you can't still build with it if you want a very distinctive look. The downside of sculk is that it's not very reflective, and so even with plenty of lighting around it can still be somewhat gloomy whenever you're close. The upside of finding it on your travels is that the usual mobs won't spawn in the surrounding Deep Darkness, but the Warden just might...

SCULK CATALYST

SCULK SENSOR

Sculk catalyst: These are more white than green, and act to spread the sculk around if any mobs are killed within its radius.

Sculk sensor: These blocks act as an alarm system, and will light up blue and emit a noise when they sense any kind of vibration. You can avoid triggering them by sneaking, although they're otherwise harmless unless there are sculk shriekers around...

Sculk shriekers: Triggered either by direct contact or any nearby noisy sensors, the shrieker will emit an alert – also seen visibly by the rings coming from it. The Warden will emerge after hearing four of these, so tread very carefully!

SCULK SHRIEKER

ANCIENT CITIES

The ultimate find in any Deep Dark biome is an ancient city. As the name suggests, this is a large area containing many simple structures with something of a Mayan flair, and a good number of loot chests and some unique rewards. Unfortunately, it will also be home to a large number of sculk sensors and shriekers, which means you can all-too easily beckon that most unwanted guest.

TIP!
Given the increased risk of bumping into an angry Warden, it makes sense to build a mini-base or two with respawn beds nearby before heading into an ancient city.

However, if you take your time and move slowly – and, most importantly, quietly – there are lots of different items and blocks decorating the city that you can mine, including the likes of soul sand, soul fire and skeleton skulls. You should also find a good number of loot chests scattered around, along with some hidden basements underneath the main palace ruins offering up even more very welcome rewards for your trouble.

If the Warden does make an appearance just be sure to steer clear of any more sensors or shriekers until it's gone! Simply standing still at a safe distance should be enough, and it's usually not worth taking any risks unless you have to. Although the addition of the echo shards and recovery compass, will make it easier to find any dropped items if you do fall to its wrath!

Ancient city or not, any Deep Dark area is one to approach with caution – but that risk/reward factor is half the fun!

TIP!
Villagers see you more as a potential leader (or trader), so they don't seem to mind when you take their stuff. Whether you want to be the kind of person that steals from them is up to you!

TREASURE HUNTING

You can mine and craft as much as you like, but there's also some great loot out there ready for the taking if you know what to look for...

GENERAL EXPLORATION

Although there are several great locations for finding some of the best in-game gear, they can be hard to find. Some of the easier ways to add to your inventory can be found on your everyday travels, such as the many villages that you'll find scattered around your world. They won't house much that's game-changing, but you can help yourself to some crops for food, some useful items from any chests you find (with the loot often related to the profession of the villager who owns it), plus maybe a free bed and shelter for the night!

If you're mining underground, you can also keep an eye out for spawner cages. As the name suggests, these small fiery crates spawn angry mobs, so tread carefully and be ready for a fight, but you can destroy the spawner with a pickaxe and will usually find a couple of chests stashed away nearby.

GOLD MINES

A far more profitable underground location to be on the lookout for are the pre-built mineshafts, complete with tunnel networks and even minecart rails. These can expand across huge distances, and are often packed with varying loot chests containing valuable armour sets, enchanted items and books, and other great stuff to make your life a whole lot easier. Plus, you should also find a good supply of ore and rails in the tunnels, along with lots of wooden planks – which is a very useful resource when you're a long way from any nearby trees.

TIP: The badlands biome has mineshafts on all levels, making it far easier to find an entrance on the surface without having to go digging underground.

EPIC LOOT

Although mineshaft locations can be great for filling up a chest or three with some really good loot, some of the best hauls can be found in those harder-to-find places. These include the likes of underground strongholds and ancient cities, which will house a good number of chests that can contain some crucial items for advancing your game (such as Nether world fortresses where you can find some of the key items you'll need to reach the End) – but they may also be home to a good number of enemies, so don't head inside unless you're well equipped for combat.

TREASURE MAPS

THE X FACTOR...

You can find treasure maps on deserted shipwrecks, which you'll mostly find underwater but can be buried on a beach if you're lucky. Inside you'll find chests with some useful loot but also a locator map that highlights both your position and a nearby X. As with all good treasure maps, X marks the spot, so simply head in its direction until you reach the location. These treasure chests are usually buried quite close to the surface, but the X can be a little vague, so you might need to dig around a fairly large area until you find it, but the rewards are usually worth the effort.

TIP: One of the main loot items you should find by following a treasure map, is a heart of the sea, which is a key component for building the conduit that lets you breathe underwater.

THE WITHER

Minecraft's first real boss fight is one you can face on your own terms, but you'll still want to be very well prepared...

PLAN AHEAD

The upside here is that you can spawn the Wither wherever you like – you just need to place four blocks of soul sand/soil in a 'T' shape and three wither skulls on the top (which will require a trip to the Nether).

There are good arguments for varying locations, such as using bedrock to help contain it, with underground locations also stopping it from flying too far away. Whatever you choose, just don't spawn it near anything you don't want destroyed!

You'll find plenty of shortcuts or mechanisms that can help beat the Wither without too much trouble. One simple option is to

build a small room with a long narrow tunnel lined with clusters of TNT or other booby traps, then spawn the Wither in the room and back out through the tunnel – giving you some easy crossbow shots and bonus explosive damage as it burrows its way towards you.

In more general terms, once you avoid the Wither's explosive arrival you can keep your distance with a bow (ideally enchanted with Infinity for limitless arrows), and dodge its fireball attacks. At 50% health in some versions the Wither will generate a shield that repels those arrows, and also spawns wither skeletons, so you'll need to get close with a sword to finish the job – but any damage can trigger a small explosion, so don't stay too close!

DEATH STAR

The Wither can be aggressive and can dish out lots of damage, so take your time and back away to heal up when you need to. After you land the final fatal blow, it will turn white and explode in a similar way to when it first arrives, so be sure to stay well back when

it does. After dying it will drop a Nether star that can be used to make beacons, which can be a real status symbol for any serious Minecraft veteran!

TIP!
If you want to 'try before you die', you can always take a trial run in Creative Mode to see the bosses in action without risking your hard-earned inventory.

GENERAL TIPS

You'll want to have seriously upgraded your set-up before taking on either of these enemies, ideally with the likes of diamond weapons and armour (or even better netherite) enchanted

to their highest levels with the likes of Smite and Sharpness for your weapons and Protection for your armour. A good selection of food or healing potions will also be needed, plus whatever

else you're able to brew up. Be prepared to duck in and out of the fight on a regular basis in order to heal and regroup, and perhaps also to drop down some quick defences or dig a hole to

THE ENDER DRAGON

The final boss battle you'll need to beat to effectively 'complete' Survival Mode, this is the ultimate test of your skills and set-up...

HOW TO TAME YOUR DRAGON

This is the ultimate end-game boss, and can be found when you first enter the End. As mentioned previously, this strange land is accessed via a portal found in underground strongholds and opened with 12x eyes of Ender.

Beds explode in the End, so be sure to place one before jumping into the portal to give yourself a handy respawn point. Once inside, the Ender Dragon won't be too far away and will quickly begin circling around, firing out fireballs and blasts of fiery breath, so you'll need to stay on the move and use the obsidian pillars as cover.

It can also use the End crystals on the top of each pillar to heal faster than you can damage it, so your first task is to destroy each one. They're explosive, so keep your distance with a bow, using dirt blocks to make a quick 'jump and place' elevator up to the top if you need to get closer or if they're guarded by a cage, before digging a few blocks back down to dodge any damage when you shoot it. The Ender Dragon has a powerful knockback effect that can send you flying, so a good supply of Slow Falling potions and/or a Feather Falling enchantment can be very useful.

THE END CREDITS

Once the crystals are cleared, you can then use your bow to pick off the Ender Dragon from a distance, or get close with the sword when it lands on the smaller central pillar. Like the Wither it will explode upon death, dropping a largely decorative dragon egg and unlocking both the exit portal back to the Overworld and a second floating 'gateway' portal which gives you access to the wider reaches of the End. In Survival Mode, this will also trigger a credits sequence – but that doesn't mean its the end of your game...

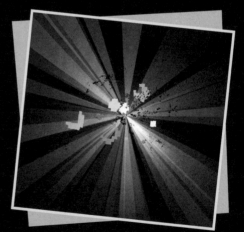

catch a breath. Both of these bosses can dish out huge amounts of damage, meaning that things can go wrong quite quickly if you're not careful, so don't rush in with kit you can't afford to lose. You should also look to set up a good mini-base or two before you get started, so you can quickly restock and get back into the fight if you do die.

TIP!
You can make Endermen ignore you by wearing a carved pumpkin on your head (though it does make it hard to see). You can also build a small army of iron golems to fight the Endermen for you!

TIP TOK

Some bite-sized nuggets of wisdom that might just help you out on your next Minecraft adventure...

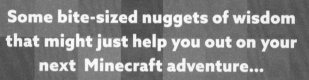

EXPLORING VILLAGES

EXPLORATION

1. You can tame a horse for a fast ride if you have a saddle, while llamas, mules and donkeys can carry chests to transport goods.
2. A quick 'elevator' can be made by jumping up and placing a new block beneath your feet, while you can also swim up and down waterfalls.
3. Build lots of mini-bases with beds and crafting tables as you travel around, so you're never too far from a safe spot to regroup or respawn.
4. Combine mining with exploration by digging upwards after a long underground trip to see where you come out!
5. As you can drop everything if you die, either travel long distances with nothing you don't want to lose, or everything you need to stay alive!

UNDERGROUND

IN THE CLOUDS

MINING

1. You don't always have to dig down. The top of rocky mountains can have large supplies of coal and iron – as well as emeralds.
2. Mobs can spawn in the underground darkness, so look to place torches to clear any new-found caves before swapping to the pickaxe.
3. Place torches or distinctive blocks, or maybe mine clean-cut tunnels, to help create recognisable paths and make it easier to find your way back home.
4. If you do get lost underground, digging up to the surface can help you spot some familiar landmarks to regain your bearings.
5. Keep a building block in your quick access inventory in case you dig into water or lava and need to hurriedly plug a hole.

DROWNED

COMBAT

1. Mobs aren't the smartest, and you can place blocks, or navigate around water and lava to keep them at a safe distance.
2. Creepers have a 3-block trigger radius and won't detonate if you're more than 7 blocks away, so hit them once and quickly back away to stop them from exploding on you.
3. The crossbow takes longer to load, but fires faster and further. However, it has a limited number of enchantment options, so a powered-up bow might still be preferable.
4. If you want a break from the action, mobs are very rare in the mushroom fields biome, so look out for the giant mushrooms to find a safe haven.
5. Equip a shield in your off-hand and use the sneak button to lift it up in order to block skeleton arrows, and even deflect them straight back.

SURVIVAL SKILLS

1. Fish can make for an endless food supply if you're near water, and it's even easier to catch them when it's raining.
2. Using shears will get you more wool from a sheep than killing it, giving you a renewable source that's handy for making beds or some colourful dyed blocks.
3. You can get milk from cows and goats using a bucket, which can then be used as an instant cure from most status effects.
4. Don't forget you can mine tree leaves to get saplings that you can plant to grow more trees and maintain a sustainable source of wood near any base.
5. You can create a limitless water supply with just two full buckets! Simply dig a 2x2 square (1 block deep), then empty a bucket into diagonally opposite corners and the water flow system will be able to constantly top up the hole.
6. Cats and ocelots scare away creepers, so adopting a few as pets can keep your home base that little bit safer...
7. ... or you can build iron golems using iron ingots and carved pumpkins to create your own army of protectors!

WATER SUPPLY

CATS

45

20 QUESTIONS

Put your Minecraft mastery to the test with this craft-y quiz – although if you've been paying attention to the preceding pages, then it should be easier than mining sand with a diamond shovel!

01

Which is NOT a common name for a core edition of the game?

A) Bedrock
B) Java
C) Blockchain

02

What's the best material for weapons and armour?

A) Netherite
B) Iron
C) Gold

03

Why are beds useful?

A) Sleeping through the night
B) Acting as a respawn point
C) Both of the above!

04

What should you use to repair enchanted items?

A) Cartography table
B) Anvil
C) Furnace

05

What favourite food do cows and sheep both enjoy?

A) Carrots
B) Wheat
C) Potatoes

06

What's the magic blue ingredient required to enchant items?

A) Lapis lazuli
B) Redstone
C) Diamond

07

What is NOT a unique feature of the recent Frog arrivals?

A) Spawning tadpoles rather than infants
B) Create froglights
C) Eat creepers

08

Where might you find an allay caged up?

A) A village town hall
B) A pillager outpost
C) An underground stronghold

09

What BBC TV show can you also explore in Minecraft Education Edition?

A) Frozen Planet II
B) Horrible Histories
C) Blue Peter

10

What's the name of the new enchantment for moving quickly while crouched?

A) Swift Sneak
B) Creepy Crawl
C) Speedy Feet

11

What is the in-game Marketplace currency called?

A) Mojang money
B) Minecoin
C) Crafty cash

12

Which biome is the best place to find pre-built minecart tunnels?

A) Underwater
B) Snowy plains
C) Badlands

13

What special food type provides bonus hearts AND health regeneration?

A) Golden apple
B) Chorus fruit
C) Suspicious stew

14

What is the best type of track to give your minecart a speed boost?

A) Activator rail
B) Powered rail
C) Towel rail

15

What new trick can you do with mangrove tree saplings?

A) Eat them
B) Grow faster
C) Plant them underwater

16

What type of sculk block will alert the Warden to your presence?

A) Shrieker
B) Catalyst
C) Sensor

17

What is a common reward for following a treasure map to its loot chest?

A) Heart of a lion
B) Heart of the sea
C) Heart of gold

18

What blocks do you need to build a portal to the Nether?

A) Cobblestone
B) Obsidian
C) Andesite

19

What can be used as a quick cure for most status effects?

A) Bucket of tadpoles
B) Bucket of lava
C) Bucket of milk

20

What's the title of the all-new addition to the Minecraft family?

A) Minecraft Legends
B) Minecraft Heroes
C) Minecraft Mobs

To find out how you got on, turn to page 48 for the answers!

Answers

Page 18-19

MONSTER HUNT

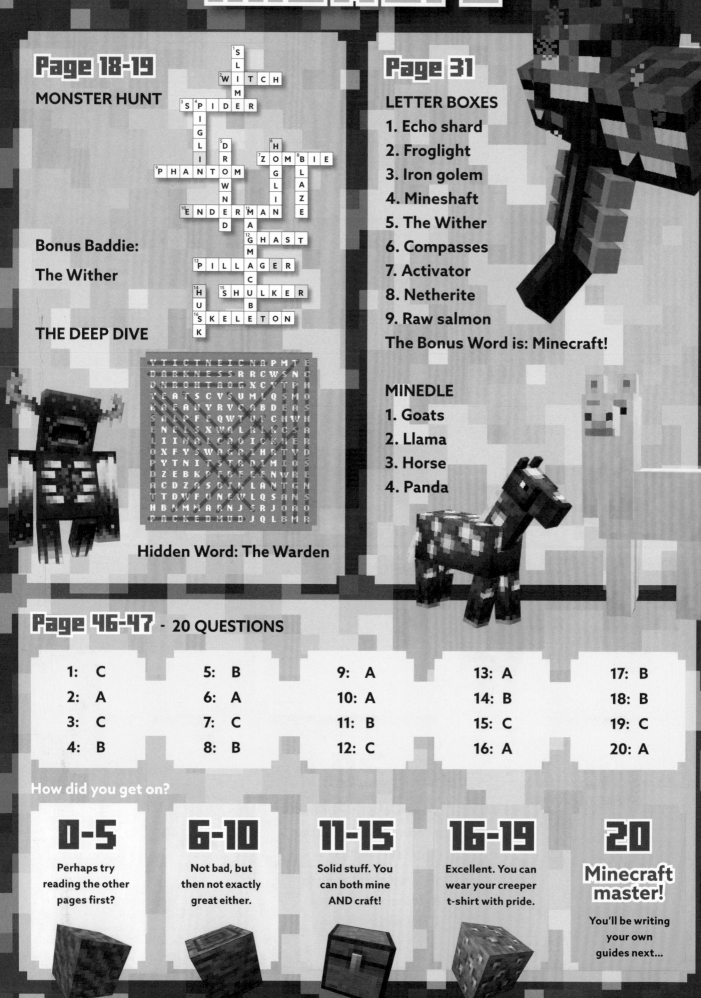

Crossword answers:
- S L I M E
- W I T C H
- S P I D E R
- P I G L I N
- D R O W N
- H O G L I N
- Z O M B I E
- P H A N T O M
- B L A Z E
- E N D E R M A N
- G H A S T
- P I L L A G E R
- H U S K
- S H U L K E R
- S K E L E T O N

Bonus Baddie:

The Wither

THE DEEP DIVE

Word search grid:

```
Y T I C T N E I C N A P M T E
D A R K N E S S R R C W S N C
D N R O H T A O G X C Y T P H
T E A T S C V S U M L Q S M O
R O E A N Y R V C A B D E A S
S A L P F E Q W T U F C H W H
E N E L S X W A L A L K C S A
L I I N B L C A O I C K N E R
O X F Y S W A G R I H R T V D
P Y T N I T S T B D I M I O S
D Z E B K P F G E E E N W R E
A C D Z A S D I K L A N T G N
T T D W F U N E W L Q S A N S
H B M M A R N J S R J O A O
P A C K E D M U D J Q L B M R
```

Hidden Word: The Warden

Page 31

LETTER BOXES

1. Echo shard
2. Froglight
3. Iron golem
4. Mineshaft
5. The Wither
6. Compasses
7. Activator
8. Netherite
9. Raw salmon

The Bonus Word is: Minecraft!

MINEDLE

1. Goats
2. Llama
3. Horse
4. Panda

Page 46-47 - 20 QUESTIONS

1: C	5: B	9: A	13: A	17: B
2: A	6: A	10: A	14: B	18: B
3: C	7: C	11: B	15: C	19: C
4: B	8: B	12: C	16: A	20: A

How did you get on?

0-5
Perhaps try reading the other pages first?

6-10
Not bad, but then not exactly great either.

11-15
Solid stuff. You can both mine AND craft!

16-19
Excellent. You can wear your creeper t-shirt with pride.

20
Minecraft master!
You'll be writing your own guides next...